Wild Life LOL!™

Goats

G.O.A.T. stands for Greatest of All Time!

SCHOLASTIC

Library of Congress Cataloging-in-Publication Data
Names: Cohn, Jessica, author.
Title: Goats/by Jessica Cohn.
Description: New York: Children's Press, an imprint of Scholastic Inc., 2020. | Series: Wild life lol! | Includes index. | Audience: Grades 2-3 | Summary: "Book introduces the reader to goats"—Provided by publisher.
Identifiers: LCCN 2019027469 | ISBN 9780531129784 (library binding) | ISBN 9780531132654 (paperback)
Subjects: LCSH: Goats—Juvenile literature.
Classification: LCC SF383.35 .C64 2020 | DDC 599.64/8—dc23
LC record available at https://lccn.loc.gov/2019027469

Produced by Spooky Cheetah Press

Book design by Kimberly Shake. Original series design by Anna Tunick Tabachnik.

Contributing Editor and Jokester: Pamela Chanko

Printed in Heshan, China 62

SCHOLASTIC, CHILDREN'S PRESS, WILD LIFE LOL!™, and associated logos are trademarks and/or registered trademarks of Scholastic Inc.

1 2 3 4 5 6 7 8 9 10 R 29 28 27 26 25 24 23 22 21 20

Scholastic Inc., 557 Broadway, New York, NY 10012.

Photographs ©: cover, spine: Susan Rydberg/iStockphoto; cover speech bubbles and throughout: Astarina/Shutterstock; cover speech bubbles and throughout: pijama61/Getty Images; back cover: Sergey Tsvetkov/Dreamstime; 1: katrin88888/Shutterstock; 3 top: Dr. Neil Overy/Science Source; 3 bottom: Gerard Lacz/age fotostock; 4: JimSchemel/Getty Images; 5 left: All-Silhouettes.com; 5 center: Vectorig/iStockphoto; 5 right: Potapov Alexander/Shutterstock; 6-7: Olivier Born/Minden Pictures; 8-9: NHPA/Superstock; 10-11: yavuz sariyildiz/Getty Images; 11 inset: Sumio Harada/Minden Pictures; 12-13: Winfried Wisniewski/Minden Pictures; 14-15: Peter Mooij/Alamy Images; 16 top: David & Micha Sheldon/Getty Images; 16 bottom: Ljkamler/Dreamstime; 17 top: Monty Rakusen/Getty Images; 17 bottom: dmaroscar/iStockphoto; 18: Juniors/Superstock; 19 left: Johner Images/Getty Images; 19 right: John E Marriott/All Canada Photos/age fotostock; 20: Anna Konchits/Dreamstime; 21 top left: FotoFlirt/Alamy Images; 21 top right: Bob Gibbons/Minden Pictures; 21 bottom left: Essence Photograph/Shutterstock; 21 bottom right: Shannon Krohn/EyeEm/Getty Images; 22-23: Bernd Rohrschneider/FLPA/Science Source; 24: alecsps/Shutterstock; 25 left: Robert Eyers/iStockphoto; 25 right: Quirky images of people and places N.America and Europe/Getty Images; 26 left: Johner Images/Getty Images; 26 right: Interim Archives/Getty Images; 27 left: John Eveson/Minden Pictures; 27 right: Pilar Azaña Talán/Getty Images; 28 left: FLPA/Alamy Images; 28-29 top: Anankkml/Dreamstime; 28-29 bottom: Erni/Shutterstock; 29 top right: southtownboy/iStockphoto; 29 center: photomaster/Shutterstock; 29 bottom right: Dr. Neil Overy/Science Source; 30 map: Jim McMahon/Mapman ®; 30 inset: yavuz sariyildiz/Getty Images; 31: Scott Madaras/Dreamstime; 32: Geraint Rowland Photography/Getty Images.

TABLE OF CONTENTS

Ready, set, GOAT!

MEET THE MIGHTY GOAT

Are you ready to be amazed and amused? Keep reading! This book will give you lots to chew on.

LOL!
What did the goat say when it was late for school? Sorry! Time GOAT away from me!

HAY there!

At a Glance

Where do they live? → Goats live in forests, in grasslands, and on hillsides. They also live on farms.

What do they do? → Goats spend most of the day looking for food and eating.

What do they eat? → Goats are fond of grass, but they also like moss and other plants.

What do they look like? → Goats have horns that grow away from the face, and their feet have hooves.

How big are they? →

HINT: It depends on the goat!

Human (age 9)

Boer goat (adult)

Nigerian dwarf goat (adult)

64 lb.

340 lb.

75 lb.

GOATS IN THE WILD

Goats are social animals.
They live in groups called herds.

THAT'S EXTREME!
Wild goat herds can have up to 500 members.

Home, Sweet Home
There are nine main kinds of wild goats. They live in the Middle East and Central and South Asia.

habitat: the place where a plant or an animal makes its home

Count on It

The size of a goat herd depends on the **habitat**. A herd that lives in open grassland may have hundreds of members. Herds are smaller in areas that are thick with plants.

WACKY FACT: U.S. Rocky Mountain "goats" are not really goats. They belong to a different family.

Good Night, Goats

At night, wild goats rest in spots where they will be hidden from **predators** like wolves or bears.

predators: animals that hunt other animals for food

A GOAT'S BODY

Goats may be yellow, brown, tan, or black.

Horns of Plenty

Most male and female goats grow horns. The horns are covered with the same material that's in your nails.

THAT'S EXTREME!
A goat's horns can be up to 4 feet wide from end to end!

Hair to Help

Some goats have short hair. Others have long hair that people clip off to make yarn for sweaters.

Now, Hear This

Goats' ears are not one-size-fits-all. Some goats have small ears. Some have ears that are big and droopy.

Eye See You

A goat can see nearly all around its body without moving! People can only see about halfway around when standing still.

EXPERT CLIMBERS

Goats are built for climbing. If they need to, they can go to great heights!

Balancing Act

A goat bends its elbows in toward its body's center to balance while climbing.

Shoulders Above

A goat has strong muscles in its shoulders and neck. That gives the goat extra climbing power.

THAT'S EXTREME!
In Morocco, goats often climb argan trees to nibble on a favorite fruit.

LOL!
What do mountain climbers tell around the campfire? **GOAT stories!**

Get a Grip

Each hoof has two parts that can separate a bit. It's kind of like having two toes. This helps a goat keep its grip.

Rock Steady

Claws called dewclaws grow at the back of each ankle. The dewclaws help goats stay steady.

THE WORLD OF GOATS

Long ago, wild goats were taken in and raised to live with people.

Old Goats
Remains of the **ancestors** of today's goats were left in ancient settlements. Goats may have been the first animals to be raised by humans.

ancestors: family members who lived long ago

You HERD It Here

People started to raise goats for their milk, meat, hides, and hair. Raising goats is also called herding.

One Big Family

More than 200 **breeds** of goats live with people around the world.

WACKY FACT: People have long used goat poop, called dung, for fuel. They dry and burn it.

breeds: living things with similar looks and ways

FARM GOATS

Today, most of the world's goats have been **domesticated**.

Goats Everywhere
Domestic goats live all over the world, in almost every place people live.

FAST FACT:
Goats get sad if raised alone.

domesticated: tamed in order to live with people

GOATS AT WORK

Goats are super helpful. Here are just some of the things they can do.

Landscapers

Some companies rent out goats to clear forest floors. This can help prevent forest fires.

Load Lighteners

Goats carry food and gear. People get goats to help them when they explore the wild.

We HERD you need help!

You GOAT it!

Milk Buds

Goats also give us milk. Their milk is used to make cheese, yogurt, and ice cream.

Don't Sweat It

Some goats have coats that are good for making warm, soft sweaters. To gather the wool, the goat's undercoat is combed off.

GOATS ARE SMART!

Goats **communicate** with their keepers to get what they want.

THAT'S EXTREME!
Researchers showed goats pictures of people. When given a choice, the animals chose photos showing happy people.

WACKY FACT:
Goats can follow the direction a person is pointing to.

So Tricky!

Goats can come when called if they are taught their names. They can learn to heel, walk, and play dead, too!

communicate: to share information

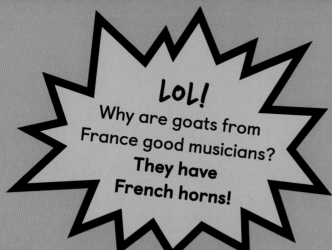

No Problem!

Researchers gave some goats a test. The goats had to figure out how to get fruit from a box by pulling a rope. They solved the puzzle—and got their treat!

Pretty Please?

Goats know how to beg with their eyes! When a goat's food is covered, the animal will look a person in the eye until he or she gets the food out.

ON THE MENU

A curious goat will chew on your shirt! But for meals, a goat likes **vegetation**. It can eat more than 5 pounds of plants a day!

THAT'S EXTREME!
A goat has four stomachs! Food moves through them in stages.

WACKY FACT:
Goats don't have top front teeth. Their food gets broken down in their stomachs.

LOL!
Why did the farmer put the goat in charge? **She was an expert in her field!**

I always LEAF room for dessert.

vegetation: plant life

grass

shrubs

These are some of a goat's favorite foods in the wild.

tree bark

twigs

STARTING FAMILIES

A female goat is called a doe or a nanny. A doe is ready to **mate** at about seven months old.

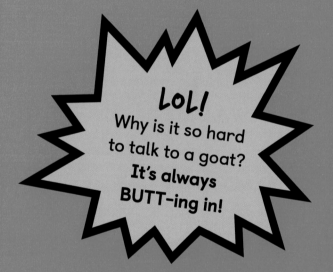

LOL!
Why is it so hard to talk to a goat?
It's always BUTT-ing in!

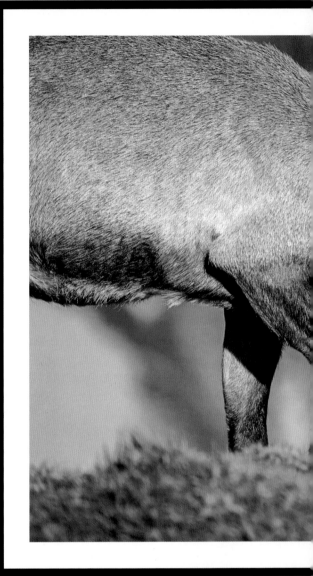

1

Butt Out!
Goats that are ready to mate hit other goats with the tops of their heads. This is called butting.

mate: to join together to have babies

THAT'S EXTREME! Goats usually have more than one baby at a time. The world record is seven!

Ouch! Quit poking me!

2

The Challenge

A male goat is called a billy or a buck. Males fight each other for the right to mate with a doe.

3

Babies on Board

After the doe mates, her babies start to grow in her belly. In about 150 days, they will be ready to be born.

ONE OF THE KIDS

Goats are **mammals** that have babies called kids. Giving birth is called kidding.

THAT'S EXTREME!
A kid can stand up and walk very soon after it is born!

WACKY FACT:
Little goats have been called kids for centuries—long before young humans were.

Hungry Kids

The kids drink their mother's milk for four to eight weeks. At around one month old, the kids learn to eat hay.

mammals: animals that produce milk to feed their young

Maa, Is That You?

Moms have a special bleat that's only for their own kids. The babies can recognize their mom's call from far away.

What a Grind!

Kids get eight baby teeth in their first four weeks. The first two of 32 adult teeth show up at about age one.

GOATS AND PEOPLE

People have kept goats for a long time!

12,000 years ago

People in the Middle East started to keep goats. Goats are very hardy. The animals were able to thrive even in the hot desert.

1500s

Spanish explorers brought the first goats with them when they visited North America. The animals were taken along to provide food and milk.

THAT'S EXTREME!
Legend says goats discovered coffee. Long ago, a herder in Africa tried fruit from a coffee tree after his goats ate it!

WACKY FACT:
Many people who get sick from cows' milk can drink goats' milk.

Today

There are nearly 400,000 U.S. milk goats. The state of Wisconsin has the most. California has the second-highest number of milk goats.

Looking ahead

Most species of wild goats are under threat. For example, the population of the Cretan ibex has decreased dramatically. They will need our help to survive!

Goat Cousins

Goats are part of a big family of mammals with horns and hooves. Here are some other family members.

wildebeests

Tibetan antelope

We live in Asia.

We're famous for our curling horns.

bighorn sheep

Please note: Animals are not shown to scale.

The Wild Life

Domesticated goats live all over the world. Their numbers are growing. But wild goats, which live in the red areas on this map—parts of the Middle East and Central and South Asia—are under threat. How can we help protect them for years to come?

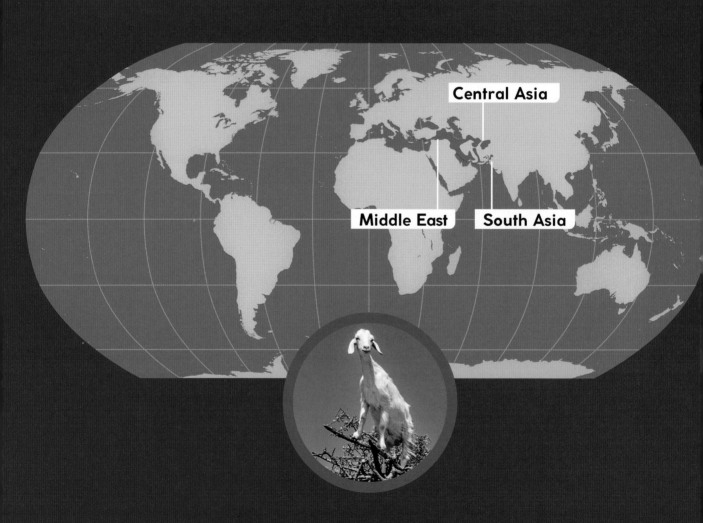

Central Asia

Middle East

South Asia

Goat Threats

The temperature on Earth is rising. It tends to be warmer around the world than it used to be. That makes it difficult for plants and animals to continue to thrive. People are building in areas that were meadows and grasslands. As wild goat habitats shrink, so do their numbers.

The loss of plants, wild goats, and their relatives is a problem for our planet! Wild goats need to be able to find food to keep having kids. If fewer kids are born each year, the population will shrink.

What Can You Do?

Talk to an adult about supporting the wild goats and their relatives. Pay attention and follow news about projects that help these animals around the world. You can adopt a wild animal by contacting Defenders of Wildlife or the Wildlife Conservation Society. Have a "Greatest of All Time" bake sale. You can help wild goats and their relatives by raising money and awareness.

INDEX

ABOUT THE AUTHOR

Jessica Cohn has written more than 50 books for children. The research she did for this book was one of her favorite assignments ever. In California, where the author lives, goats "mow" the grass in some of the parks. She's a big fan of goats and all they do for us.

GOAT to run!